MW00981302

N

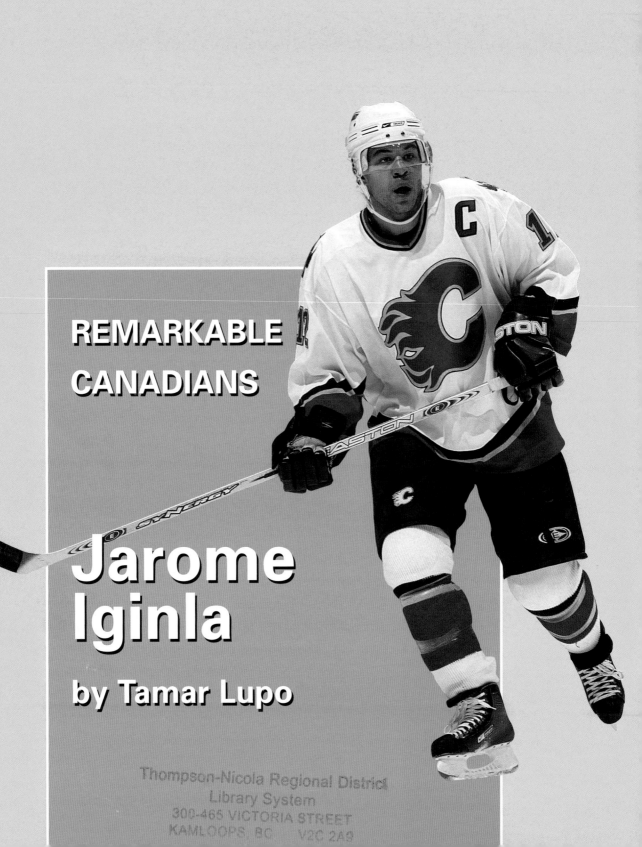

REMARKABLE CANADIANS

Jarome Iginla

by Tamar Lupo

Published by Weigl Educational Publishers Limited
6325 – 10 Street SE
Calgary, Alberta, Canada
T2H 2Z9

Website: www.weigl.com

Library and Archives Canada Cataloguing in Publication

Lupo, Tamar
        Jarome Iginla / Tamar Lupo.

(Remarkable Canadians)
Includes index.
ISBN 978-1-55388-313-5 (bound).--ISBN 978-1-55388-314-2 (pbk.)
        1. Iginla, Jarome, 1977- --Juvenile literature.
2. Calgary Flames (Hockey team)--Biography--Juvenile literature.
3. Hockey players--Canada--Biography--Juvenile literature.
I. Title. II. Series.

GV848.5.I35L86 2007   j796.962092   C2007-900887-9

Printed in the United States of America
1 2 3 4 5 6 7 8 9 0 11 10 09 08 07

Editor: Liz Brown
Design: Terry Paulhus

We acknowledge the financial support of the Government of Canada through the Book
Publishing Industry Development Program (BPIDP) for our publishing activities.

Cover: Jarome Iginla is captain of the Calgary Flames hockey team.

Photograph Credits
CP (Dean Bicknell): page 19; Courtesy of Jarome Iginla: page 8.

Every reasonable effort has been made to trace ownership and to obtain permission
to reprint copyright material. The publishers would be pleased to have any errors
or omissions brought to their attention so that they may be corrected in
subsequent printings.

Contents

Who Is Jarome Iginla?

Jarome Iginla is a hockey player. He is the captain of a hockey team called the Calgary Flames. The Flames are part of the National Hockey League (NHL). Jarome is only the second player of African **descent** to be the captain of an NHL team. In 2002, Jarome became the first NHL player of African descent to win the Art Ross Trophy and the Maurice "Rocket" Richard Trophy. These awards are given for point and goal scoring achievements in the NHL. Jarome also helped the Canadian men's hockey team win the gold medal at the 2002 winter Olympics in Salt Lake City, Utah. Jarome is well known because of hockey and his work in the community.

"People say confidence is overstated, but I don't think so..."

Growing Up

On July 1, 1977, Jarome Arthur-Leigh Adekunle Tig Junior Elvis Iginla was born in Edmonton, Alberta. Jarome's father, Adekunle "Elvis" Iginla, is from Nigeria. Jarome's mother's name is Susan Schuchard. She is from Medford, Oregon.

When Jarome was two years old, his parents divorced. He and his mother moved to St. Albert, a town outside of Edmonton. Jarome saw his father often. In St. Albert, Jarome lived near his grandparents. They often took care of him while his mother was at work.

As a child, Jarome liked to watch hockey. He admired the Edmonton Oilers, a hockey team in the NHL. He liked Oilers players such as Wayne Gretzky and Mark Messier. His favourite player was Grant Fuhr. Grant Fuhr played **goalie** for the Oilers. Jarome admired Grant for his hockey skills and because they shared an African **heritage**.

🍁 When Jarome was a child, the Edmonton Oilers won five Stanley Cups.

Alberta Tidbits

COAT OF ARMS

TREE
Lodgepole Pine

FLOWER
Wild Rose

Edmonton is the capital of Alberta.

Alberta entered **Confederation** on September 1, 1905.

Banff National Park is in Alberta.

More than three million people live in Alberta.

Calgary and Edmonton are the largest cities in the province.

Think about it!

Alberta is the province where Jarome Iginla was born. It is the province where he lives today. Research Alberta's hockey history. How might hockey players from the past, such as Fuhr and Gretzky, have influenced Jarome's career?

Practice Makes Perfect

Jarome began playing sports at age six. He played tennis, baseball, and bowling. When Jarome was seven years old, his grandfather signed him up for a hockey league.

At first, Jarome played goalie because his favourite player was a goalie. Later, Jarome played **forward**. He discovered that he was good at scoring goals, so he kept playing forward.

When Jarome was nine years old, he told his mother that he wanted to be a **professional** hockey player. He began working hard to achieve this dream.

🍁 Jarome was good at many sports and won several trophies and medals when he was young.

In 1991, Jarome began playing for the St. Albert Eagle Raiders in the Alberta "AAA" Midget Hockey League (AMHL). This is a league for Alberta's best hockey players who are younger than 17 years old. In the AMHL, people began to notice Jarome's talent. Between 1992 and 1993, Jarome was the leading goal scorer in the AMHL. He scored 87 points during the season.

QUICK FACTS

- Jarome's last name means "big tree" in Yoruba. Yoruba is his father's native language.

- Jarome was good at music when he was a child. He played the piano and recorder.

- Jarome's mother sang the national anthem at his games with the St. Albert Eagle Raiders.

That autumn, Jarome was asked to play in the Western Hockey League (WHL) for the Kamloops Blazers. The WHL is a Canadian hockey league for players 20 years of age and younger.

Jarome had to play in many other hockey leagues before he became an NHL player.

In 1993, Jarome moved to British Columbia to play for the Kamloops Blazers. At first, the coaches did not give him much ice time. This is because they wanted Jarome to learn from the more experienced players. When the Blazers made the **playoffs**, Jarome began to play more often. In his first year with the Blazers, Jarome scored nine points in 19 playoff games. This helped the Blazers win the 1994 Memorial Cup. The Memorial Cup is the championship trophy for the WHL. In 1995, Jarome and the Blazers won the Memorial Cup again. That year, the NHL's Dallas Stars **drafted** Jarome. A few months later, he was traded to the Calgary Flames.

For the next six years, Jarome improved his skills in the NHL. In 2001, he was invited to play for Team Canada at the 2002 Olympics in Salt Lake City. In the gold medal game against the United States, Jarome scored two goals. Canada won the Olympic gold medal. Jarome became a hockey hero.

Jarome never played a game with the Dallas Stars. He was traded to the Calgary Flames before the hockey season began.

Thoughts from Jarome

Jarome's love of sports and dedication to hockey led him to a **career** in the NHL. Here are some things he has said about his life and work.

Jarome talks about being a hockey player of African heritage and being a role model.

"It meant a lot to me that Grant Fuhr was playing right there in Edmonton... I'm glad if I can be a role model. I know what it meant to me."

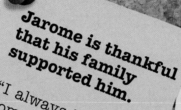

Jarome is thankful that his family supported him.

"I always had somebody in the stands. I always had somebody there."

Jarome believes all children should have the chance to play sports.

"I believe that everyone should have the opportunity to participate and experience the many benefits that sports provide."

As a child, Jarome was full of energy.

"Back then, I was exhaustingly energetic, so my mom got me into everything—bowling, little league, tennis, you name it."

Jarome talks about winning the gold medal at the 2002 Olympics.

"The game was so intense. I didn't think about winning or losing until the last three minutes. That's when I thought, 'we're going to have this.' It was just the best feeling."

Jarome improves his skills while playing for Team Canada.

"...Being out there with the best players in the game...it helped my confidence."

What Is a Hockey Player?

Jarome is a hockey player. A hockey player is an athlete who plays on a hockey team. A hockey team needs to have at least six players. On the ice, there is one goalie, one right **wing**, one left wing, a **center**, and two **defense** players. Jarome's position is right wing.

Hockey is played on an ice rink. Two teams play against each other. The players on one team try to get a puck into the other team's net. They skate on the ice, using a long stick to move the puck. A hockey game is 60 minutes long. It is divided into three 20-minute periods, or sections of time.

Hockey players can play the game as a hobby, or they can play hockey as a career, like Jarome does. Hockey players who choose to play hockey as a career play in professional hockey leagues, such as the NHL.

A hockey team needs to have extra players so the players can rest during the game.

Hockey Players 101

Jacques Plante (1929–1986)

Position Goalie

Achievements Jacques Plante began playing in the NHL in 1952. The first team he played for was the Montreal Canadiens. In 1959, Jacques began wearing a goalie mask. He is remembered as the first goalie in the NHL to regularly wear a mask.

Awards Vezina Trophy, 1956–1960, 1962, 1969; **inducted** into the Canadian Hockey Hall of Fame, 1978.

Wayne Gretzky (1961–)

Position Center

Achievements Wayne Gretzky is considered one of the greatest hockey players in history. He has been nicknamed "The Great One." Wayne holds the record for the most goals ever scored in the NHL. During his career, he scored 894 goals. Wayne played for the Edmonton Oilers from 1978 to 1988.

Awards Hart Memorial Trophy, 1980–1987 and 1989; inducted into the Hockey Hall of Fame, 1999.

Bobby Orr (1948–)

Position Defense

Achievements Bobby Orr changed the way that hockey was played in the NHL. He often scored goals and helped the **offensive** players on his team. This was not something defensive players often did.

Awards Hart Trophy 1970–1972; inducted into the Hockey Hall of Fame, 1979.

Mario Lemieux (1965–)

Position Center

Achievements Mario Lemieux began his NHL career in 1984 with the Pittsburgh Penguins. Mario helped the Penguins win the Stanley Cup in 1991 and 1992. In 1993, Mario was diagnosed with Hodgkin's Disease. He took one year off from playing hockey, but he returned in 1995.

Awards Hart Trophy, 1988, 1993, 1996; Conn Smythe Trophy, 1991, 1992; inducted into the Hockey Hall of Fame, 1997.

The Hockey Helmet

In the past, hockey players did not always wear helmets. Many players suffered serious head injuries because of this. In the 1970s, the NHL made a rule that any players joining the league after June 1, 1979, had to wear a helmet. Players who were already in the NHL could choose if they wanted to wear a helmet. The last person to play without a helmet in the NHL was Craig MacTavish, who retired in 1997.

Influences

There are many people who influenced Jarome's life and career as a hockey player. Jarome's family and other hockey players were the biggest influences in his life.

Jarome's mother, Susan, supported her son. She worked many hours so that she could have enough money to pay for Jarome to play hockey. This taught Jarome about the importance of helping family. Today, Jarome helps his mother. He has paid for her to attend university at the University of Alberta.

🍁 The support Jarome received from his family helped him to achieve success in the NHL.

Jarome's grandfather, Rick, influenced him. Rick taught Jarome how to play baseball and hockey. Jarome's grandparents drove him to many of his hockey practices and games, and they always watched him play.

Other hockey players of African descent influenced Jarome. When Jarome was young, other children told him that there were not many players of African heritage in the NHL. Players such as Grant Fuhr, Claude Vilgrain, and Tony McKegney showed Jarome that a hockey player's heritage does not affect the way he plays the game.

Grant Fuhr

Grant Fuhr was born in Spruce Grove, Alberta, in 1962. In the 1980s, he played for the Edmonton Oilers. Between 1984 and 1990, Grant helped the Oilers win five Stanley Cups. In the 1983–84 hockey season, Grant earned 14 points. This is the most points ever earned by an NHL goalie in a single season.

🍁 Grant was inducted into the Hockey Hall of Fame in 2003.

Overcoming Obstacles

Jarome Iginla has experienced much success in his career as a hockey player. However, Jarome had to overcome obstacles to achieve his dream of playing in the NHL.

When Jarome played hockey as a child, he experienced **racism**. Other hockey players would sometimes call him names because of the colour of his skin. Jarome's mother, Susan, taught him to ignore this and focus on the game of hockey instead.

Jarome was not always one of the best players on his team. It took some time before Jarome was a good player for the Kamloops Blazers. When Jarome first joined the Blazers, he told his grandfather that he wanted

to leave Kamloops and move home. Jarome's grandfather told him to not give up on his dream. Jarome continued to play for the Kamloops Blazers. The coaches noticed that Jarome was improving, and they began to give him more playing time during games.

Jarome's dedication to hockey has helped him win many championships. In 2004, he was part of Team Canada in the World Cup of Hockey tournament. Canada won the World Cup on September 14.

As an NHL player, Jarome faced other obstacles. NHL coaches told him that he did not skate fast enough. To improve his speed, Jarome spent many hours working with a trainer named Lou Edwards. Jarome worked on his strength and flexibility with Rich Hesketh. Hesketh is a trainer as well. Working with these two trainers helped Jarome improve his skills as an NHL player.

Even though Jarome is a successful hockey player, he still spends many hours practising his hockey skills with his teammates.

Achievements and Successes

Jarome has worked hard to become a successful hockey player, and he uses his success to help others.

In 2002, Jarome helped Canada's men's hockey team win a gold medal at the winter Olympics. He scored three goals in six games. Jarome played on the Canadian Olympic team again in 2006. He was one of the alternate captains for the team.

In the NHL, Jarome has won many awards for his hockey playing skills. These include the Art Ross Trophy, the Maurice "Rocket" Richard Trophy, and the Lester B. Pearson Award. Other NHL players vote for the recipient of the Lester B. Pearson Award. This award recognizes outstanding performance in the NHL.

🍁 The 2001-2002 hockey season was Jarome's best season in the NHL. He won three NHL awards that season.

Jarome is a spokesperson for KidSport Canada. Each time he scores a goal during a Calgary Flames game, Jarome donates $1,000 to KidSport. Since he began doing this in 2000, Jarome has given $172,000 to KidSport. In 2004, the NHL awarded Jarome the NHL Foundation Award and the King Clancy Memorial Trophy. These awards are given to a player who shows leadership skills and works hard to help his community.

KidSport

KidSport raises money to help children pay for the cost of joining a sports team. The group also collects used sports equipment to give to children who cannot afford to buy their own. KidSport believes that sports teach children about co-operation, goals, and team play. To learn more about KidSport, visit www.kidsport.ca.

Each summer, Jarome Iginla runs a hockey camp in Calgary.

Write a Biography

A person's life story can be the subject of a book. This kind of book is called a biography. Biographies describe the lives of remarkable people, such as those who have achieved great success or have done important things to help others. These people may be alive today, or they may have lived many years ago. Reading a biography can help you learn more about a remarkable person.

At school, you might be asked to write a biography. First, decide who you want to write about. You can choose an athlete, such as Jarome Iginla, or any other person you find interesting. Then, find out if your library has any books about this person. Learn as much as you can about him or her. Write down the key events in this person's life. What was this person's childhood like? What has he or she accomplished? What are his or her goals? What makes this person special or unusual?

A concept web is a useful research tool. Read the questions in the following concept web. Answer the questions in your notebook. Your answers will help you write your biography.

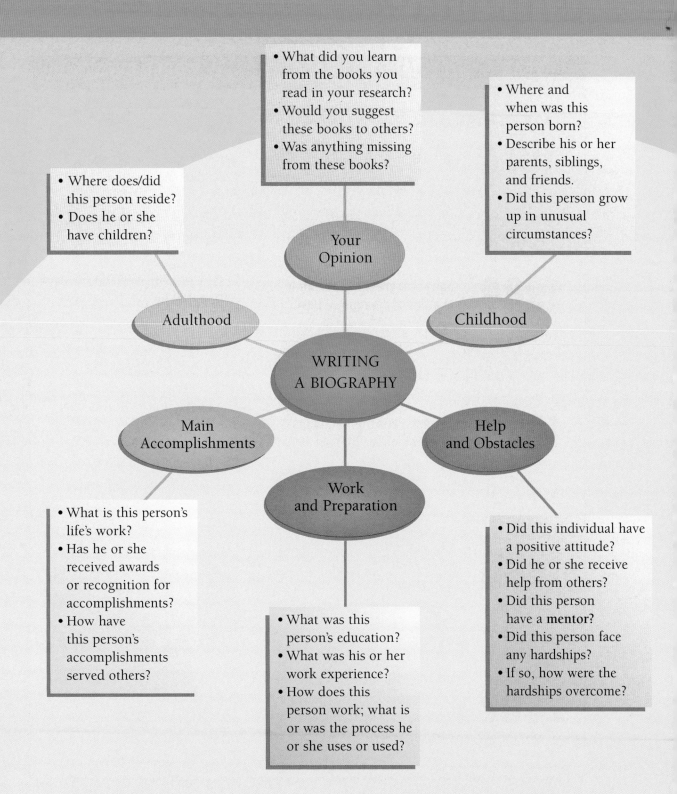

- What did you learn from the books you read in your research?
- Would you suggest these books to others?
- Was anything missing from these books?

- Where and when was this person born?
- Describe his or her parents, siblings, and friends.
- Did this person grow up in unusual circumstances?

- Where does/did this person reside?
- Does he or she have children?

Your Opinion

Adulthood

Childhood

WRITING A BIOGRAPHY

Main Accomplishments

Help and Obstacles

Work and Preparation

- What is this person's life's work?
- Has he or she received awards or recognition for accomplishments?
- How have this person's accomplishments served others?

- What was this person's education?
- What was his or her work experience?
- How does this person work; what is or was the process he or she uses or used?

- Did this individual have a positive attitude?
- Did he or she receive help from others?
- Did this person have a **mentor**?
- Did this person face any hardships?
- If so, how were the hardships overcome?

Timeline

YEAR	JAROME IGINLA	WORLD EVENTS
1977	Jarome is born on July 1, 1977.	Czechoslovakia defeats Sweden at the Men's World Hockey Championship in 1977.
1984	Jarome's grandfather enrols him in a hockey league in 1984.	Wayne Gretzky wins the Art Ross Trophy and the Hart Memorial Trophy in 1984.
1993	Jarome joins the Kamloops Blazers hockey team in 1993.	The Mighty Ducks of Anaheim, who are now known as the Anaheim Ducks, play their first NHL game in 1993.
1995	The Dallas Stars draft Jarome in 1995. A few months later, he is traded to the Calgary Flames.	Canada wins the Junior Men's World Hockey Championship in 1995.
2002	Jarome helps Canada's men's hockey team win the gold medal at the 2002 winter Olympics in Salt Lake City.	The Detroit Red Wings win the Stanley Cup in 2002.

Further Research

How can I find out more about Jarome Iginla?

Most libraries have computers that connect to a database for researching information. If you input a key word, you will be provided with a list of books in the library that contain information on that topic. Non-fiction books are arranged numerically, using their call number. Fiction books are organized alphabetically by the author's last name.

Websites

To learn more about Jarome Iginla, visit www.nhl.com. Click on "Players," and type "Jarome Iginla" into the search engine.

To learn more about the Calgary Flames, visit www.calgaryflames.com.

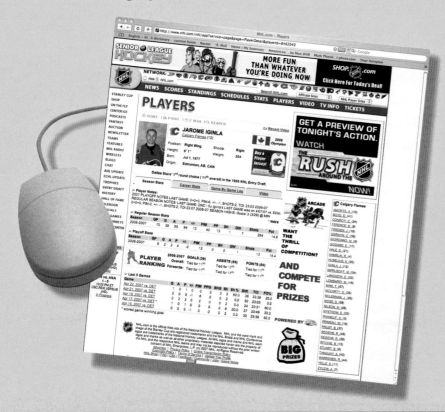

Words to Know

career: the work a person does for money

center: the hockey player who takes face-offs

Confederation: the creation of Canada in 1867

defense: players on a team whose job it is to stop the other team from scoring goals

descent: background or heritage of a person

drafted: selected to play on a hockey team

forward: an offensive player in hockey

goalie: a hockey player whose job is to stop pucks from entering the net

heritage: a person's history and traditions

inducted: admitted into a group

mentor: a wise and trusted teacher

offensive: part of a hockey team whose job is to score goals

playoffs: a series of games played to determine the winner of a championship

professional: a person who is paid to play sports

racism: treating people poorly because of their cultural heritage

wing: an offensive player whose zone of play is on the outer sides of the ice rink

Index